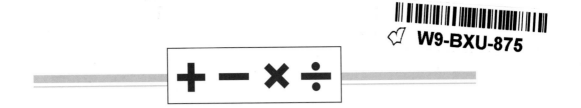

# Teaching Thinking
# and
# Problem Solving
# in Math

# by Char Forsten

SCHOLASTIC
PROFESSIONAL BOOKS

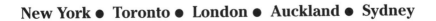

New York ● Toronto ● London ● Auckland ● Sydney

Design by Francis Klaess
Cover design by Vincent Ceci
Illustrations by Arnie Ten
"Different Dogs" by Corey Edelkind
"Joe's Summer Job" by Liz Lawler

ISBN 0-590-49171-7

Printed in the U.S.A.

To my father—who taught me
to look at life from many angles

# CONTENTS

# INTRODUCTION

## "People don't seem to realize that it takes time and effort and preparation to think."

*– Bertrand Russell*

*Please think!* Does this well-intentioned reminder sound familiar? If you are a teacher, perhaps you find yourself uttering this command to students in much the same way you ask them to sharpen their pencils or clean their desks. During my first few years in teaching, I routinely instructed students to think, assuming it was an innate skill they could turn on or off like a light bulb. I believed it would simply happen on command, and that any lack of thinking on their part was due to a shortage of motivation or a variety of external circumstances.

My thoughts on "thinking" changed dramatically one day when students were working on story problems in math. As we reviewed their solutions, not only were many responses incorrect, but they were also quite illogical. Their mathematical computations were correct, but regrettably, the calculations had little to do with the questions in the problems. When I asked students to explain how they arrived at their answers, one child proudly volunteered that he had multiplied the numbers in the problem, because after all, we were studying multiplication! I did not ask the students any further questions, but instead, posed a crucial one to myself: How could I teach the students to think so they could apply their computational skills effectively in math? Beyond that, how could I help students solve problems throughout the curriculum and in their everyday lives?

The time had come to stop asking students to think, and instead, to teach them how. Problem solving needed to become our focus in math.

I had lengthy discussions with the kids about thinking, because I wanted to give them a mind-set for our new mission. Our motto became, "It's the thought that counts!" I pored through catalogues and ordered materials that offered activities to develop thinking and problem solving abilities. I began reading the few books I could find on the topic.

Also, at about the same time, I embarked on an M.B.A. program at night. As I contemplated the students' thinking, my own thought processes were being stretched in a challenging way. In my courses, application was the name of the game, and it was accomplished through a case study approach.

One day, as I prepared to teach a math lesson, I sketched a quick case study for my own students, using a real-life situation written at their level. Guiding them through the process was a teacher's delight. Not only did they have to listen and compute carefully, but they were required to identify issues, recommend logical alternatives, and then decide on a plan of action.

These case studies, or "guided thinking activities" as I call them, became weekly activities. The whole group was actively involved in analytical and computational thinking. Soon, students asked to write their own cases, and their writing process incorporated a mathematical dimension. The teaching of thinking and problem solving techniques became critical components of my core program.

I found, however, that I needed to back up and include more steps in the process. After further research, I developed a problem solving model and have now devoted a great deal of time to teaching a variety of problem solving strategies. What has evolved is a two-tier math program. I teach computation, but devote most of my time to applying these skills through problem solving. I begin the year by developing thinking skills, then the problem solving model is introduced and separate strategies are taught. During the last quarter of the year, the focus is on applying everything learned to date by solving the case studies at the end of the book.

This book is an attempt to share what I have learned about teaching kids to think and solve problems. I will address different types of thinking, including critical, creative, and analytical, and a variety of problem solving strategies will be presented along with specific ways they can be taught to students. The book includes some examples of guided thinking activities, or case studies, and offers suggestions to the teacher on how to implement them.

The main emphasis of this book, however, is thinking and math. The book explains problem solving and the application of computational skills. It's also about critical literacy, reading and listening, discriminating information, writing, and working in groups. The problem solving model and guided thinking activities in the form of case studies can supplement most, if not all, math programs being used throughout the country. The model exemplifies what the National Council of Teachers of Mathematics has stated in *Curriculum and Evaluation Standards for School Mathematics:* that "problem solving should be the central focus of the mathematics curriculum."[1]

The examples provided in the book should give you ideas to make up problems that are appropriate for your class. Problem solving is not an "add on," but rather a "turn on." In an effective math program, I have found it to be critical. What do you think?

1. *Curriculum and Evaluation Standards for School Mathematics.* (Reston, VA: National Council of Teachers of Mathematics, 1989), p. 23.

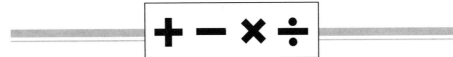

## CHAPTER ONE

# GETTING READY FOR PROBLEM SOLVING

## Changing Old Ideas About Mathematics

Emily's panic-stricken face looked up at me before she had even finished reading the problem I distributed to the class.

"I can't do this," she announced in a bewildered voice.
"Can't do what?" I asked.
"This problem," she said. "I don't get it. Could you give me some real math?"

Real math? What she wanted was an arithmetic problem. One that she could compute immediately—a problem with one correct answer. I couldn't blame her. I had not taken the time to expand her notion of mathematics, nor had I given her a mind-set for problem solving.

Emily's distress haunted me all day. I had journeyed into problem solving without adequately preparing the students for the trip. I gave them directions, but didn't teach them about the new culture they would find in the land of problem solving. As a teacher, I had learned a valuable lesson from my students. I knew I needed to back up and deal with attitudes and perceptions about mathematics.

Before beginning actual problem solving, there were three objectives I wanted to work toward with the kids. First, it was important to develop an understanding, a liking, and an appreciation of mathematics. Next, I wanted to introduce them to different types of thinking and help them realize it takes time to study information and process their thoughts. Finally, it was crucial that students accept the idea that more than one correct answer is sometimes possible in problem solving, especially when dealing with real-life issues.

## Arithmetic: Only a Part of Math

How do many elementary students view mathematics? Their perceptions remind me of a wonderful folktale from India called "The Blind Men and the Elephant." In the story, six blind men had heard many fascinating stories about the elephant and longed to know what one was like. By chance, an elephant came down the road one day. The blind men approached the animal, and each touched a different part of its huge body.

When the men gathered afterward, they eagerly described the elephant, each basing his description on the part he had touched. One blind man, who had grabbed its tail, said the elephant reminded him of a rope. Another depicted it as a tree trunk because he had grasped its leg. Still another compared it to a fan since he had taken hold of its ear. Each man had a different image of the elephant. Their perceptions were limited because their contact with the animal was restricted.

Much like in the folktale, many elementary students have a restricted view of mathematics. Is it so surprising that they see math as arithmetic, when computation has been the primary focus of the curriculum for many of them? Speaking as someone with fourteen years of classroom experience, I know the many constraints we face as teachers. In this highly technological age, it is difficult to fit everything into the school day. There are so many computational skills students must learn and teaching them takes time.

What can be done? Students should learn that the computational skills of arithmetic are tools to be used in problem solving. Arithmetic is only one part of the mathematical picture. Number concept, measurement, geometry, patterns and their relationships, statistics, probability, estimation, and logical reasoning all partake of skills learned in arithmetic.

Addition, subtraction, multiplication, division, fractions, and decimals are arithmetic skills best introduced in a meaningful context. When initially teaching each operation, look around the classroom for examples of problems to create. For example, when beginning multiplication, ask students how they might figure out the number of shoes being worn in the room without using addition. They ought to suggest that each person has two feet; therefore, two times the number of people in the room would give you the total number of shoes.

Once students demonstrate an understanding of the concept and the algorithm, assign practice problems for homework. Use most of the precious classroom time for problem solving, putting the skills to work.

## Making Math Fun

It is also important to break down the "proverbial math block." Sometimes the mere mention of the word "math" triggers an "I can't do it" response. There are ways to take the mystery out of mathematics. Humor is a real tension breaker in many situations, but is especially helpful in math. In the classroom, positive attitudes can be nurtured by beginning each lesson with a math riddle. Include the students when possible or use funny names in your riddles. An example might be:

**If Mary Land is two years older than Ari Zona, and Ari's age is the same as a prime number between six and ten, how old is Mary?**

Once students become accustomed to solving riddles, they love to write their own. It's a refreshing change for them to create challenging and fun math mind joggers during their writing time.

## Developing an Appreciation for Math

A "Math Appreciation Day" at the beginning of the school year can help raise students' level of consciousness about the presence of math in their everyday lives. A walking field trip to find math in the environment may produce symmetry in leaves, geometric shapes in buildings, and patterns in windows and other objects along the way.

Proportion can be examined between buildings and people, or trees and shrubs. Consider the probability of a particular type of vehicle passing. What are the odds that a truck will pass? Estimate how long it will take for a light to change, then actually time it. Estimate the length of the playground in yards, then check it.

Pick up litter along your walk, estimate its weight, then check it on a scale. Examine the litter and discuss what you can learn from the trash left behind. Were there many smokers, or candy bar eaters, or soda drinkers? What are the more common types of litter? Try graphing your findings.

Use your walking trip to sensitize students to their surroundings. Have fun asking questions about what you find along the way, even though there are no obvious answers.

Make students aware that math is not something they simply learn at school. Without even thinking, they use it throughout the day. Have the children ask their parents or other adults how they use math at home and work. Talk about different professions and the types of math needed to do the jobs. Find as many ways as you can to help students appreciate math and understand its importance in their daily lives.

## *Thinking Takes Time*

In the Introduction, I shared my realization that thinking needs to be taught and developed. Thinking also takes time. Many students feel the need to respond immediately to every question the teacher asks.

Try posing an open-ended question such as: "If you could spend one day with anyone alive today, which person would you choose?" Tell the class to think and not raise their hands for three minutes. When the time is up, ask not only for responses to the question, but also inquire how it felt to wait. How many changed their minds? How many felt impatient?

For some students a waiting period can seem like an eternity, and they remain focused on their initial thoughts, waiting for the time to be up. But with practice, students should learn to do productive thinking and consider a variety of possibilities before making a final decision.

To reinforce that ideas take time to develop, I rely on Thomas Edison to help make a point. I ask students if they think Thomas Edison woke up one day and decided that he would invent the light bulb. Did he simply gather the materials he knew he needed, and without hesitation, make the first light bulb?

Some laugh, while others are not sure. Children are accustomed to seeing finished products. They have not witnessed the thinking and trial and error process that began with an idea and ended in a product.

We must give students time and permission to think. Edison's remark, "Genius is one percent inspiration and ninety-nine percent perspiration," provides an excellent springboard for a discussion on productive thinking. Learning from mistakes, not quitting or making the same error repeatedly, takes willpower and effort. But then Edison also believed, "There is no substitute for hard work," a useful motto for today's students who may be accustomed to immediate gratification. Of course, students will probably acknowledge that some situations require a great deal of thinking, and others, very little. To contrast problems that take a short time for thinking as opposed to those that take longer, put two columns on the board and ask the students to brainstorm examples for each:

| Short-term Thinking | Long-term Thinking |
| --- | --- |
| What to eat for breakfast | Planning weekly meals |
| What to do on Saturday | Where to go on vacation |
| What to play with a friend | How to build a clubhouse |

Students should begin to generalize that the more complex the task, the more thinking time necessary.

## Three Kinds of Thinking

Like it or not, we make dozens of decisions throughout the day. So many, in fact, we simply aren't conscious of each and every one we make. Something I share with students is that we use different kinds of thinking when we deal with problems.

**1. Analytical or investigative thinking** is what we use when we examine a problem and figure out how to solve it. We use available information to arrive at a logical conclusion. This type of thinking incorporates mathematical thinking. Analogies, inference activities, and other word games help students learn to analyze.

**2. Creative thinking** takes place when we suggest possible alternatives. Open-ended questions help develop creative thinkers by encouraging a variety of solutions to the same problem. Students begin looking at the world around them in new ways, and learn to accept a range of differing opinions. Brainstorming and inventions are just two ways that allow kids to broaden their creative horizons.

**3. Critical thinking** involves an educated opinion about a situation. Critical thinking is not responding negatively, but rather is an evaluative type of response where a student uses facts and logic to back up his or her opinion of a situation. In this setting, having an opinion is not valid unless it is supported by credible facts and logical thinking. Class debates or persuasive writing are ways to foster critical thinking in the classroom.

As you pose questions throughout the day, help students recognize which thought approaches they are using. Some will find they are great analytical thinkers, but are hesitant to offer ideas for new ways of doing things. Others might be reluctant to give their opinion of a situation. To develop all types of thinking, it takes time and requires a safe environment—one where risk taking is encouraged and mistakes are considered part of the learning process.

### APPROACHES TO A PROBLEM USING THE THREE KINDS OF THINKING

| Problem | What's the best way to arrange students' desks? |
|---|---|
| **Analytical** | What is the pattern of desks used in the classroom? |
| **Creative** | What are other possible seating patterns that could work in the room? |
| **Critical** | What is your opinion of the seating pattern in the room? Why do you think it will or will not work? |

## More than One Correct Answer

When I began teaching problem solving, I found many students uncomfortable with the idea that there might be more than one correct answer. Arithmetic exercises and story problems that reinforce computational skills do have only one possible response. Open-ended problems, however, such as naming many different workable seating arrangements for a classroom, have a variety of alternatives. Analytical, creative, and critical thinking all come into play with open-ended problems such as this one: *What would you do if you each had an extra ten dollars?* Ask this question, and you will probably get as many answers as there are students. Analytical and creative thinking are taking place. From a different perspective ask, *What should be done with ten dollars, so the entire class benefits?* Different conditions and varied opinions bring critical thinking into the picture.

Real-life problems have more than one answer. Of course, some answers are better than others, which is why it is so important that students learn to be critical thinkers.

Just as problems can have more than one answer, stretch students' minds by showing them that answers can have more than one problem, too. To get them thinking, tell the class: The answer is 20. There are innumerable problems to go with it. Students might offer anything from 18 + 2, to the square root of 400, to a story problem that leads to an answer of 20. A good method to use with this activity is webbing:

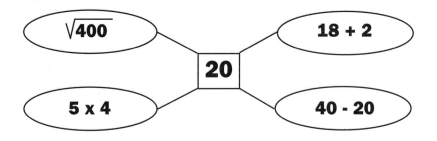

There is much we can do to make math exciting and meaningful for children. And the future workplace will surely benefit from students who not only have been well-trained in academics, but who also have been challenged to analyze and resolve creatively a variety of problems and situations throughout their school careers.

Getting ready for problem solving requires creating a positive mind-set with students. But there are other factors to consider before starting.

## Creating a Classroom Environment Conducive to Problem Solving

"Math counts" is a message I want to convey to those entering my classroom. A classroom environment that stresses the importance of math shows kids the priority status of math in their lives. Hands-on materials and visual aids that stimulate thinking encourage students to solve problems individually or in groups during their free time.

What can be done in the classroom? A wide selection of manipulatives should be available for student use. Building blocks, Lego, Pattern Blocks, tangrams, Cuisenaire Rods, UNIFIX Cubes, Attribute Blocks, Geoblocks, dominoes, and a variety of recyclables all provide hands-on experiences for students. Experimenting with these materials allows children the opportunity to learn through exploration and trial and error.

Another way to foster curiosity and thinking is to post a "Problem of the Day or Week." This device has been a favorite with my students; they love the challenge of figuring out the math mystery of the day. Daily or weekly puzzles can be teacher-made or purchased from various educational publishers, such as Dale Seymour or Dandy Lion.

Visual aids that stimulate thinking or serve as reminders should be displayed in the room. Prints such as those by M.C. Escher are excellent visual resources to hang in the room. Students are captivated by such artistic representations of mathematics.

Handmade posters promote mathematical thinking. To follow are some suggested messages.

**POSTERS PROMOTING MATHEMATICAL THINKING:**

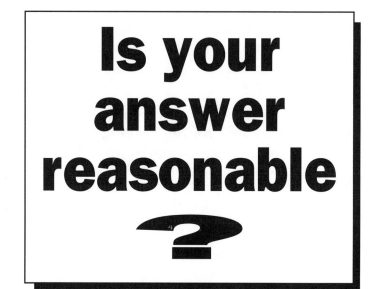

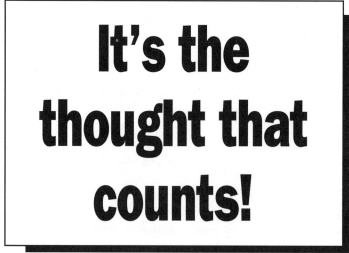

*POSTERS FOCUSING ON KEY WORDS TO OPERATIONS:*

# ADDITION

- sum
- all
- together
- total
- in all
- altogether

# SUBTRACTION

- difference
- left
- less than
- How many more?
- fewer than
- greater than
- more than
- How many less?

# MULTIPLICATION

- product
- in all
- times
- all
- If each one cost $5, how much will 10 cost?

# DIVISION

- quotient
- each
- divide equally
- per
- average
- If 10 cost $50, how much will one cost?

## A POSTER OUTLINING THE STEPS TO PROBLEM SOLVING:

1. **Determine the problem.**

2. **Identify relevant facts and their relationships to each other.**

3. **Specify important conditions.**

4. **Choose a strategy.**

5. **Solve the problem.**

6. **Check your results.**

Designing posters with math slogans is a motivational math/art activity for kids. Another suggestion is bringing in photographs or magazine pictures that show patterns, shapes, proportion, and symmetry in nature. These make an excellent bulletin board where students can learn to observe the world around them with a discerning eye. Games, both student made and store bought, help reinforce math skills and promote social interaction. In my school, a volunteer comes in once a week for "Chess Club," an excellent activity that develops analytical skills and strengthens the idea that careful thinking takes time. Materials that foster positive attitudes toward problem solving and help students think mathematically should be an integral part of a math program. Visual aids displayed in the classroom serve as constant reminders that math plays a central role in our lives.

## Encouraging Parental Involvement

Recent educational articles point out that a key determinant for a child's school success is the value placed on education by the parent. How much a parent reads to a child, helps with homework, or encourages learning has a profound impact on how well the student does in school.

Experience has taught me that when a parent and teacher are in sync philosophically, the child greatly benefits. There are few mixed messages, and learning is not a phenomenon considered to happen only at school.

Parents generally support the teaching of problem solving, although they may not be familiar with the methodology themselves. Sensitivity to a parent's own comfort level with math and problem solving is an important consideration. It is critical not to make parents feel inadequate in the eyes of their children; therefore, as a teacher, I accept full responsibility for the problems I ask students to solve. I try to keep parents well informed of what I am doing and encourage their participation if they are comfortable.

For many adults, there is a vast difference between their own school days and the present. Some parents come to me and share their own difficulties when attempting to solve some of the problems, which leads to frustration for them and their child. This is counterproductive, and a reason why I spend most of the class time working on problem solving.

If problem solving is a new focus for you, there are different steps you can take to inform parents and enlist their support:

**1.** An open house at the beginning of the year is an excellent forum to walk through the children's curriculum, taking the opportunity to explain problem solving and its place in your math program.

**2.** Invite parents to sit in on a problem solving lesson, where they can see the students interact and express their thoughts.

**3.** Send home a letter explaining what problem solving is and how parents can support their child.

**4.** Ask students to write letters to their parents explaining that they will be studying problem solving strategies, and how a parent might help.

When communicating with parents, emphasize the need to guide students through their thinking when helping them, and not give them the answers to problems. Reinforce that problem solving is a process learned over a period of time, and that understanding is the key to learning, not simply completing an assignment.

I let parents know they are not expected to assist students if they are uncomfortable. Emphasize that the most important service they can provide is to give their children a supportive environment at home so that thinking can take place and homework can be completed with minimal distraction.

## Using Calculators and Computers

Problem solving allows students to apply their mathematical skills and develop their sense of logical reasoning. Because the emphasis of problem solving is on application rather than arithmetic, calculators and computers can be an integral part of the problem solving lesson.

### Do Calculators Replace Computation?

Calculators do not replace the need to know addition, subtraction, multiplication, and division. In arithmetic, the focus of the lesson is to learn to compute. In problem solving, however, the goal is to analyze a situation and know how to apply computational skills. As I mentioned earlier, a way I make time for problem solving is to assign practice problems in computation for homework. Then I can spend the bulk of class time working on more complex situations that require the application of arithmetic skills.

In addition to being highly motivational, using calculators accomplishes two objectives. It provides more time for problem solving by freeing the students to think instead of compute. It also teaches kids to use tools adults rely on regularly in real life.

During problem solving, students begin to realize that some situations call for mental math, others are better suited for paper and pencil computation, and many are best completed with the calculator. With experience, they learn to distinguish not only what to do, but the most efficient means of doing it.

In the face of tight budget constraints, how do you obtain calculators for your class? Our school was fortunate. A local business donated small solar calculators and there were enough for each student in my class to have one. When I taught students to use the calculators, this was extremely helpful. During problem solving sessions, though, one per group was adequate.

If your own school does not have funds for calculators, try approaching businesses in your area. More than ever, the business community is becoming involved with education because it realizes that its future is dependent upon the development of human potential.

## A Case for Computers

Computers, too, are excellent tools to use in problem solving. Obviously, schools vary in their ability to provide computers for younger children. There is one computer in my classroom. Students take turns using it for writing exercises, and of course they love the interactive games.

Appleworks is the word processing program we use, and the software also includes a data base and a spreadsheet section. Students use spreadsheets to record and compute average daily, weekly, and monthly temperatures. I would recommend the use of spreadsheets for academically talented students in the intermediate grades. Plugging formulas into cells on a spreadsheet can be challenging without adult instruction and supervision, but keep it in mind for those students who are ready for something extra. Perhaps a volunteer who is familiar with computers would be willing to come in and teach advanced skills to a small group of students.

I try to purchase software that encourages thinking and problem solving. There is an abundant selection from which to choose, but just a few suggestions are:

*Gertrude's Puzzles* (Learning Company) (Grades 3 – 8). Students develop reasoning skills by classifying objects and working with incomplete information to solve puzzles.

*Hands On Math, Volume 1* (Ventura) (Grades K – 7). Students explore mathematical concepts through the use of colored rods, tiles, counters, geoboards, tangrams, and chip trading.

*Hands On Math, Volume 2* (Ventura) (Grades K – 7). Two color counters, color tiles, mirrors, attribute blocks, and base ten blocks allow students to explore basic operations, probability, symmetry, place value, and logical thinking.

*Think Quick!* (Learning Company) (Grades 2 – 8). Students use critical thinking and logical reasoning to explore the Castle of Mystikar.

Peer tutoring works very well with computers. Knowledgeable students teach their classmates, and it is a wonderful opportunity for older kids to work with younger children. In fact, many students with learning disabilities or emotional difficulties have had great success with the computer, and their self-esteem improves when they help other students learn to use it.

The goal of using calculators and computers is not to replace a student's need to know basic facts and arithmetic computation. These are essential to building a strong foundation in all areas of mathematics. Too much time has been devoted solely to these skills, however, and students must learn to apply them, not just mechanically perform them. In our highly technological age, students should learn to view calculators and computers as tools that allow us to work with large amounts of information and solve a variety of complex problems.

## Cooperative Learning Groups

When students work in groups, they learn to listen and talk to each other rather than always focus on the teacher. With clear instructions and expectations, members of a group can be actively involved in the thinking process, working through the problem solving steps together and reacting to each other's thoughts and opinions.

Not to be confused with small groups, cooperative learning groups follow set guidelines where students work together, not side by side. If you are not familiar with cooperative learning groups, you may want to talk with colleagues who use it in their classrooms, or you might read literature on the method. *Cooperative Learning: Getting Started* by Susan S. Ellis and Susan F. Whalen (New York: Scholastic, 1990) is an excellent and very readable source. It explains what cooperative learning is and how to implement it in your classroom.

During problem solving, I assign students to work in heterogeneous groups of three or four. I give each group a calculator, scrap paper, and a progress chart. The chart, shown in Chapter 2 (page 37), explains how each group is to progress through the steps of the problem solving process. It also asks students to evaluate their work as a group. Specific social skills are listed on the chart and students must judge how effectively they worked together. Did they listen to each other? Did each person offer his or her opinion? Did the group come to a consensus?

In real life, it is crucial for an individual to analyze a situation and be open-minded about new solutions. Equally important is the ability to work in a group toward a common goal. If students learn important social skills at a young age, it will better prepare them to be effective citizens when they are older. When beginning group work, I always ask my students how we can expect the world to treat each other with compassion if we don't practice getting along right here in this small room.

## *Getting Started with Problem Solving*

In this chapter, the preliminaries to problem solving were addressed. Whenever you plan a trip, preparations must be made. Now that we have completed them, let's get started by moving ahead to Chapter 2 and taking a closer look at the problem solving model students will be using.

CHAPTER TWO

# GETTING STARTED BY INVESTIGATING THE PROBLEM

## What Is a Problem, Exactly?

For many of us, the word *problem* has a negative connotation. Something is wrong that needs to be fixed.

Of course, there are many cases where this is true. When your car makes a suspicious noise, you see dollar signs. At school, when two students argue, you are likely to ask, "What's the problem?"

In mathematics, a problem can be a simple algorithm waiting to be computed or a complex situation with one or more steps and calculations needing to be solved.

I tell students problems are situations that require some kind of action or they go unresolved. If I am hungry, I must decide what to eat, then actually consume the food. If I want to take a vacation, I read about possible locations, then choose one to visit and take the trip. If I face a math problem, I must understand it, decide what to do, then solve it.

A variety of cultures exist in this world because societies solve the problems of food, clothing, shelter, and rules differently. Stop and think about it. An Inuit will solve the problem of needing shelter differently than an aborigine, because the conditions they face are so dissimilar. The fact that each situation reflects different conditions makes problem solving a fascinating adventure.

It is helpful for students to have an expanded view of what a problem is, whether it is a math riddle with one possible answer, or a social issue such as the solid waste program requiring in-depth analysis.

## A Model for Problem Solving

Have you ever met someone who seems to know exactly what to do no matter how serious the problem? Such a person confronts an issue, sizes it up, and is at ease making a prompt decision. Most likely, he or she is well-trained or experienced in solving problems. We can help students feel comfortable with problem solving by starting to educate them in logical reasoning processes when they begin school.

In order to accomplish this, we must give students a sequence in which to analyze problems. Children face an overload when confronted with a task that requires them to do many things at once. Certainly complex problems can overwhelm them and leave the door open for a math block to form. That is why it is important to train students to approach problems in a step-by-step fashion.

The following is a problem solving model I use in my teaching:

1. Determine the problem.
2. Identify relevant facts and their relationships to each other.
3. Specify important conditions.
4. Choose a strategy.
5. Solve the problem.
6. Check your results.

## Step 1: Determine the Problem

Have you ever walked around with a knot in your stomach and wondered what was bothering you? You know once you figure it out, you can work it through, and be rid of that gnawing feeling.

Determining what the problem is may seem like an easy step, but we should not take for granted that students will always recognize it. This skill requires concentration on the question and the ability to create a mental image of the situation. To help determine the problem:

1. Read, and, if necessary, reread the problem.
2. Create a mental picture of the problem.
3. Find the question and put it in your own words to show understanding.

Allow time for students to practice this skill of determining the problem. By starting out with simple problems, students will be better able to analyze more complex situations.

## Step 2: Identify Relevant Facts and Their Relationships to Each Other

Math problems vary according to the amount of information they contain. Students must learn to sift through facts and decide which are necessary to solve the problem. They must also determine their relationships to each other and the order in which they will use them. We have all seen examples that contain too much information such as:

> **Terry, Larry, and Harry all collect baseball cards. Terry started with thirty-six, gave five to Larry, then bought three from her brother. Larry started with fifty-four. His brother, who collects stamps, gave him another thirteen for his collection. When Larry counted up his cards, he was very upset, because he was missing one of Reggie Jackson. He looked everywhere, but could not find it. Finally, there was Harry, who had the largest collection of seventy-two cards. Last Saturday, he went to a shop and traded three of his cards for five others. How many more cards did Harry have than Larry?**

At first glance, this problem is confusing with its rhyming names and juggling of numbers. Students not trained in problem solving are overwhelmed. Those who learn the step-by-step approach would:

**1.** Determine the problem: In the end, how many more cards did Harry have than Larry?

**2.** Identify relevant facts and their relationships to each other:

$$\text{Larry's Cards:} \quad 54 + 5 + 13 - 1 = 71$$
$$\text{Harry's Cards:} \quad 72 - 3 + 5 = 74$$

Terry's role in this situation helps students create a mental picture of the problem, and the five cards she gave to Larry must be figured into the math equation. The other number facts about Terry are irrelevant to the solution—they contribute to an understanding of the whole picture, but are not necessary to solve the problem.

Much practice is needed to identify relevant facts correctly. Many students do not have a system for analyzing problems; they manipulate the numbers, come up with an answer which may or may not be reasonable, then move on to the next order of business.

## Step 3: Specify Important Conditions

When choosing relevant facts, it is also important to identify conditions that might exist in a problem. In real life, if you want to buy a snack and only have fifty cents, you should immediately eliminate any snacks over this amount. You do not want to waste your time on solutions that are not feasible.

In Chapter Five of this book, I will explain how to do case studies with students. Recognizing conditions becomes a crucial step in these thinking activities. As children become more involved with real-life situations, they must not only look at the problem mathematically, but they also need to consider any conditions that could affect the solution.

If Billy, who is asthmatic, is groping with the dilemma of taking in a stray cat, he must consider both the cost factor of caring for the cat and the condition of his health when making his decision.

## Step 4: Choose a Strategy

A variety of strategies used in problem solving are discussed at length in Chapter Three of this book. The ones I have included are: key words to operations; guess and check; make a table or an organized list; draw a picture or use real objects; work backwards or make it simpler; find a pattern; and use logic.

I introduce each strategy separately in a large group setting, provide practice problems, then when all strategies have been taught, give students a variety of problems where they must decide what to do on their own or in their cooperative learning groups. Examples of teaching these applications are provided in Chapter Three.

### Step 5: Solve the Problem

This is straightforward—students carry out the plan. Having determined the problem, identified relevant facts and their relationships, recognized conditions, and chosen a strategy, they should now be able to solve the problem mathematically and consider important factors to come up with a logical answer.

### Step 6: Check Your Results

A few years ago, I had a conference with a parent who is also a high school math teacher. When I discussed my concerns about students' ability to think and solve problems, he told me that if we could just get kids to ask this important question: "Does the answer make sense?," it would make a tremendous difference in their progress in math.

Thus the question, "Is the answer reasonable?" became a critical part of my math lessons. Students know I am going to ask this. In fact, I have a large poster hanging on a wall that constantly poses this evaluative question to the children.

When I ask if the answer is reasonable, I am really directing them to consider whether they used the correct computational approach and backed it up with logical reasoning.

A problem that will demonstrate whether students are thinking logically is:

**There are thirteen kids in an afterschool chess club. They have been invited to a tournament on the other side of the city, and must find adults to drive them. If only four students can ride in each car, how many cars will be needed?**

I have seen answers such as 3R.1, which shows the student recognized division as the correct operation, but failed to determine the problem and understand what sort of answer was appropriate.

Other students might suggest only three cars are needed, because the one extra student could sit on someone's lap. This shows an understanding of the problem and creative thinking, but it also demonstrates the student did not recognize given conditions. The answer is not reasonable because the problem stated only four students could ride in each car.

Experience has taught me that many kids tend to use "if only" thinking. "If only the thirteenth student could sit on someone's lap, then only three cars would be needed." When this happens, I acknowledge their use of creative thinking in coming up with an alternative that would save gas and drivers, but I remind them that this problem gave the condition that only four students could ride in each car. There can be no "if only" in this case.

That is why, when dealing with logical thinking in math problems, I remind students they must recognize and adhere to given conditions.

Open-ended problems are another matter. There are times when altering conditions can be a problem. When students change variables in an experiment, they are altering conditions. In order to discover the effects of environmental factors on plant growth, students will vary the conditions in controlled experiments. Open-ended activities and real-life problems encourage students to develop all types of thinking. There are problems where conditions can be altered. Help students see how important conditions are when economists offer ways to control inflation, health workers discover cures for diseases, and environmentalists search for solutions to our solid and toxic waste problems.

When teaching problem solving to elementary students, I usually establish ground rules at the beginning of a session. Later, students are better able to determine which problems are open-ended and which require adherence to given information. When asked whether their answer is reasonable, students must be sure they have determined the correct problem, identified important facts, and recognized given conditions.

Checking results needs to become a habit.  Reward students for questioning their answers and praise their movement through each step in the problem solving process.

How can you track the students' progress or identify their weak areas in the problem solving model?  A chart that shows their thoughts at each step is a good way to observe growth.

## *Summary: Charting the Model*

As you work through the model, students can fill in a chart to check their progress in problem solving and social skills.  They can  put the entire model to use with the following problem:

> **Jack and Jill went up the hill to fetch 2 liters of water. Along the way, they met Ms. Muffet who was collecting spiders.  When they finally reached the top and filled their container with water, they turned around and began to run down the hill.  Jack fell down and spilled the water everywhere.  If Jack was 2 meters ahead of Jill, and Jill was 5 meters from the top, how far down the hill was Jack?**

The sample chart on page 37 (filled out in the name of John Doe) guides students through the six steps in the problem solving model and helps prevent them from getting stuck.

## *Learning Problem Solving Strategies*

After examining the problem solving model as a whole, it is time to focus on the step of choosing a strategy.  In Chapter 3, a variety of strategies will be presented and each will include warm-up activities, math applications, and extensions.

# Problem Solving Chart

Name: John Doe    Group: Challengers    Date: June 1

Problem: How many meters from the top of the hill was Jack?

Relevant facts: 1.) Jill was 5 meters down the hill.
2.) Jack was 2 meters farther than Jill.

Conditions: Jack was 2 meters farther down the hill than Jill. Jill was not in front of Jack.

Strategy: Draw a picture.

Jack———Jill——————top of hill
2 m.        5 m.        = 7 m.

Solution: 2 m. + 5 m. = 7 m.
Jack was 7 m. down the hill.

Reasonable answer? Yes. Jack was in front of Jill by 2 meters, which would mean he was farther down the hill.

## SOCIAL SKILLS

Contributions to group: I drew the picture.

Encouraging words: I told Jill she did a great job of finding important facts.

Ways I cooperated: I let John determine the problem, even though I wanted to do it.

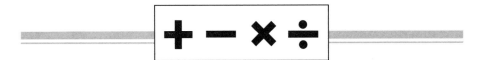

CHAPTER THREE

# UNDERSTANDING PROBLEM SOLVING STRATEGIES

## What Are Problem Solving Strategies?

I view a strategy as a specific plan of action. It shows forethought and an understanding of what to do in a situation. In mathematical problem solving, there are a number of strategies that help students find solutions. The ones included in this book are:

- locate key words to operations
- guess and check
- make a table or an organized list
- draw a picture or use real objects
- work backwards or make it simpler
- find a pattern
- use logic.

## How Are the Strategies Taught?

Now that students have developed positive mind-sets for math, engaged in a variety of thinking activities, and learned the problem solving model, I am ready to present specific methods to help them analyze problems. I compare choosing a correct strategy to a carpenter deciding which tool is needed in a particular situation. While a wrench could certainly pound in a nail, the hammer makes the job much easier.

In problem solving, I introduce each strategy separately through warm-up exercises, then math applications to provide practice and strengthen understanding of each specific method. Eventually, students work through a variety of problems where they must choose which strategy or combination of them will be most helpful in reaching a feasible solution.

The strategies are also presented separately in this section. I have included suggestions for warm-ups that get kids ready for each strategy. They can be adapted to most elementary grade levels. The math applications are problems that reinforce the use of each particular strategy. The examples are meant to provide practice for students and give you ideas on how to create your own math problems to apply each strategy. There are different levels of difficulty. This allows you as a teacher to decide which problems are appropriate for your own class. Extensions are also included should you wish to go beyond the practice problems.

## Key Words to Operations

Probably the most common type of story problem in the elementary grades is the kind that requires simple computation involving one or two steps. The students must choose the correct arithmetic operation to solve the problem. Since certain words or phrases provide clues to either addition, subtraction, multiplication, or division, students learn to identify key words.

### Warm-up

**Earning a Ps.D.:** When teaching how to use key words, I tell students they will try to earn a Ps.D (Doctor of Problem Solving). We actually become math surgeons who must decide which arithmetic operation to perform based on the "symptoms" or clues in the problem.

The symptoms are the key words to the four arithmetic operations, which I have written on individual posters and displayed on the wall, as shown in Chapter One. Some of the key words are:

**Addition:** sum; altogether; in all; total; plus

**Subtraction:** difference; left; minus; fewer than; less than; greater than; more than; How much change?; How many less?; How many more?

**Multiplication:** product; altogether; in all; times; If one costs $5, how much will four cost?

**Division:** quotient; divided equally; in each; per; average; If four cost $20, how much will one cost?

I usually begin by discussing how doctors use symptoms to identify and treat health problems. Then I tell students to pretend they are studying to be math doctors and to use key words as symptoms to identify which arithmetic operations to perform.

I demonstrate with an exaggerated example such as: *If I went to the doctor and complained of a swollen ankle, would I feel better if he bandaged my ear?* Of course, they think that is quite silly; the doctor did not use the symptoms to treat the problem.

Then I ask students what would happen if they performed the wrong mathematical operation on a problem. What happens when you add, but should have subtracted? I remind students that just as doctors do not take their professions lightly, nor should they as mathematicians. It is critical that they become literate in math terminology and think about the words that suggest specific operations.

Use the key word posters to make up simple problems for the children to diagnose which arithmetic operations are required. When you call on students, refer to them as doctors, such as Doctor Smith or Doctor Jones.

This motivational warm-up helps students think about the connections between words and math operations. Learning key words is the foundation to building literacy with an increasing number of math terms.

## *Applications*

### Making doctor rounds

Problems involving computation and key words are in most if not all math textbooks. It is not necessary to provide sample problems, but what I do with students is make "doctor rounds." When we are working on story problems in math, we form a team to examine the problem, determine the key words, then perform the math operations. We always check to make sure we have given our patient (the problem) the correct treatment by rereading the questions and determining that the answers are reasonable.

## Extensions

**1. Writing process:** During writing time, have students write their own math problems that include key words. Ask students to exchange problems when they are finished.

**2. Crossword puzzle:** Make a crossword puzzle where the key words are the clues for the operations.

**3. Math dictionaries:** Provide notebooks where students put one letter of the alphabet on the top of each page. As students learn new math terms or phrases, they can enter them alphabetically in their dictionaries.

## Guess and Check

Many students are not skilled in making educated guesses. We recognize that most of our great inventions came through trial and error, but we do not encourage this skill in the classroom. The guess and check method follows this sequence:

1. Make an educated guess.
2. Try solving the problem.
3. Make a better guess based on what you learned in the first trial. Each guess should become more educated and lead you closer to the solution.
4. Use the guess and check technique until the problem is solved.

### Warm-ups

**1. Hot/cold game:** In this game, the teacher or a student chooses an item in the room and keeps it a secret. Students may then ask if it is a particular object: "Is it the globe?" If it is far away from the chosen article, the response given is "cold." If it is close, on the other hand, the answer given is "hot." Classmates take turns guessing what the item is until someone identifies it. Each response should become better educated as it gets closer and closer to the real thing.

**2. How much?  How many?:** Set up an estimating center each day. Place items such as a bowl of raisin bran, a jar of marbles, or a dish of pretzels on a table.  Place a class list next to the item where students can mark their estimates under a column labeled "There are about ??? items today."  For the bowl of raisin bran, students might approximate how many raisins are in the bowl.  At the end of the day, check to see who came closest to the exact number.

**3. Telephone book math:** This could be a center or a cooperative learning activity.  A number is given by the teacher, and students must find a telephone number whose sum of digits equals the given number. For example, if 24 is named, a number such as 566-2131 is an acceptable response (5+6+6+2+1+3+1=24).  Students should write down the full name and telephone number to check their results.

## *Applications*

**1. Guesstimating:** Ask students to "guesstimate" how many marbles, crayons, or other common objects are in a see-through container.  After each student's initial response has been recorded on the board, empty out about half of the items for students to count.  Once students know how many fill approximately half of the container, give them a chance to make a second, more educated guess.  Write their second response next to their first one for comparison.  Count the items left in the container and add the number to the first half to get a total sum.  Decide who the "Guesstimater of the Day" is and discuss the conclusions.

**2. Guess and measure:** Answer the following questions by first writing down an educated guess, then checking your results:

  **a.** How many feet can you jump?
  **b**. How many dominoes will fit along the length of your
      desk?  The entire perimeter?
  **c.** How many times do you breathe in fifteen seconds?
  **d.** How long is a minute? (This is a partner activity where one
      student estimates, while the other records the actual time.)
  **e.** How many teaspoons of water will fit into a cup?

**3. Making equations:** Insert the correct arithmetic signs that will make the following equations true:

| | | |
|---|---|---|
| **a.** 7   2    2    = 3 | ( 7 - 2 - 2 = 3) |
| **b.** 6   2    4    = 4 | ( 6 + 2 - 4 = 4) |
| **c.** 3   7    4   20 = 5 | ( 3 x 7 + 4 - 20 = 5) |
| **d.** 30  (6  3)    = 12 | ( 30 - (6 x 3) = 12) |
| **e.** 7  7  (8  2) 3  = 30 | ( 7 x 7 - (8 x 2) - 3 = 30) |

Insert numbers that will make these equations true:

**f.** _____ + _____ - _____ = 10    (answers vary)

**g.** _____ x _____ + _____ = 20    (answers vary)

**h.** _____ - _____ x _____ - _____ = 40    (answers vary)

**4. Name the coins:** What are the coins?

**a.** I have 3 coins that total $ .16.    (1 dime, 1 nickel, 1 penny)

**b.** I have 4 coins that total $ .41.    ( 1 quarter, 1 dime, 1 nickel, 1 penny)

**c.** I have 6 coins that total $ .41.    (3 dimes, 2 nickels, 1 penny)

**d.** I have 8 coins that total $1.56.    (6 quarters, 1 nickel, 1 penny)

**e.** I have 9 coins that total $1.00.    (1 quarter, 7 dimes, 1 nickel)

**5. Find the numbers:** What are the numbers in question?

**a.** Jill and Will are sister and brother. If Jill is 2 years older than Will and their ages add up to 36, how old is Jill?

| | 1ST GUESS | 2ND GUESS |
|---|---|---|
| JILL | 18 | 19 |
| WILL | 18 | 17 |
| TOTAL 36? | YES | YES← |
| IS JILL 2>WILL | NO | YES← |

**b.** Freddie Freeloader loves cookies. He decided to fill up his bag with chocolate chip and peanut butter cookies. If the total number he could fit in the bag was 34 and there were 12 more peanut butter cookies than chocolate chip, how many of each kind were in the bag?

*Sample Solution:*

| | 1ST GUESS | 2ND GUESS | 3RD GUESS |
|---|---|---|---|
| PEANUT BUTTER | 26 | 25 | 23 |
| CHOCOLATE CHIP | 14 | 13 | 11 |
| TOTAL 34? | NO | NO | YES← |
| PB 12>CC? | YES | YES | YES← |

## Extensions

**1. Shopping trip:** This is an estimating exercise. Obtain permission from a local store for a volunteer to take a small number of students on a math field trip. Have them locate different numbers of items that total

46

$5.00 by rounding off the prices. No pencil and paper or calculators, please.

**2. Catalogue/newspaper math:** Set up a learning center with a catalogue or newspaper ads where students choose items to purchase for different amounts of money. Have them round off their prices and their totals.

**3. Investigating probability:** Ask what is most likely to happen in the following situations:

   **a.** If I have 2 red jellybeans and 6 green jellybeans in a bag, which color am I most likely to pick out? (green)
   **b.** If I have 5 yellow M&Ms and 5 brown M&Ms, which color am I most likely to pick out? (There's an equal chance of choosing either color.)
   **c.** If I have 1 green ball and 4 red balls in a bag, what are the odds I will pick out the green ball? (1 in 5)

## *Make a Table or an Organized List*

Making a table or an organized list helps students sort numerical data into a meaningful structure. When tables or lists are made, solutions are more obvious because they are found in a systematic way. Tables and lists organize information that would be too difficult for students to track mentally.

Tables and charts are used to put facts or figures in an orderly sequence. An example familiar to most students is a multiplication table, which is a grid that can be used to determine both multiplication and division facts. The following example illustrates how a table can be useful in problem solving:

**Sue and Drew are sisters. Sue is 3 years old and Drew is 5. How old will both girls be when the sum of the digits in both their ages is 8 again?**

| SUE | DREW | SUM OF DIGITS |
|---|---|---|
| 4 | 6 | 10 |
| 5 | 7 | 12 |
| 6 | 8 | 14 |
| 7 | 9 | 16 |
| 8 | 10 | 9 |
| 9 | 11 | 11 |
| 10 | 12 | 4 |
| 11 | 13 | 6 |
| →12 | 14 | 8 (1+2+1+4) ← |

The table allows a student to see readily that Sue would be 12 and Drew would be 14, because 1 + 2 + 1 + 4 = 8. An organized list is quite similar to a table, except it is generally used to organize information to find possible combinations of given items in a problem. An example of this strategy is as follows:

**Sam loves cats and dogs. His mother told him he could adopt one cat and one dog from the Humane Society. When Sam arrived to choose his pets, he found a tabby, a tiger, and a Persian cat in the room. When he visited the dogs, a beagle, a terrier, and a poodle all looked at him longingly. Since Sam can only choose one cat and one dog, what are the possible combinations of pets he might adopt?**

*Sample Solution:*

TABBY/BEAGLE    TIGER/BEAGLE    PERSIAN/BEAGLE
TABBY/TERRIER   TIGER/TERRIER   PERSIAN/TERRIER
TABBY/POODLE    TIGER/POODLE    PERSIAN/POODLE

Making an organized list allows students to see all possible combinations presented in an organized fashion.

## Warm-ups

**1. How many ways?:** How many ways can students . . .

    **a.** walk from their desks to the door?

    **b.** walk or ride from their homes to the school?

    **c.** line up in a group of 3? (6)

    **d.** stack four different books in one pile? (24)

    **e.** spell other words from letters in their own names?

**2. Pizza combinations:** Obtain a pizza menu from a local pizzeria. Using the menu, have students work in cooperative learning groups to find as many triple topping combinations as possible.

**3. What's your favorite?:** Introduce or review bar graphs with students. Brainstorm topics of favorite things that can be plotted on graphs, such as: colors, books, authors, movies, vegetables, meats, fruits, desserts, beverages, ice cream, yogurt, snacks, etc. Assign partners and ask students to . . .

    **a.** choose their topics

    **b.** poll their classmates

    **c.** use the data to graph their results.

Display the graphs on a bulletin board entitled: "These are a few of our favorite things."

## Applications

**1. Find the number:** Sue and Lu are 2 and 5 years old. What will their ages be when the sum of their digits is again 7?

| SUE | LU | SUM OF DIGITS |
|-----|-----|-----|
| 3 | 6 | 9 |
| 4 | 7 | 11 |
| 5 | 8 | 13 |
| 6 | 9 | 15 |
| 7 | 10 | 8 |
| 8 | 11 | 10 |
| 9 | 12 | 12 |
| 10 | 13 | 5 |
| →11 | 14 | 7 (1+1+1+4=7)← |

**2. Find the number:** Tom Foolery loves riddles and can never give a simple answer. One day his teacher asked how many pages he had read in his book over the weekend. Tom told his teacher he had read more than 50, but fewer than 100. He also said the number could be divided evenly by 5 and 15 and 25, and that if you count by fives, you will say the number. How many pages did Tom read over the weekend?

*Sample Solution:*

Divisible by
5 & 15 & 25?

| 50 | 55 | 60 | 65 | 70 | 75 | 80 | 85 | 90 | 95 | 100 |
|----|----|----|----|----|----|----|----|----|----|-----|
| N | N | N | N | N | Y | | | | | |

**3. Find the combinations:** List the different numerals you can make from the following digits:

**a.**  2 & 4          (2 combinations: 24, 42)
**b.**  3, 5, & 7      (6 combinations: 357, 375, 537, 573, 735, 753)
**c.**  1, 6, 8, & 9   (24 combinations: 1689, 1698, 1869, 1896, 1968,
                       1986, 6189, 6198, 6819, 6891, 6918, 6981, 8169, 8196,
                       8619, 8691, 8916, 8961, 9168, 9186, 9618, 9681, 9816, 9861)

**4. Find the combinations:** Lisa has a new baby brother and is helping her family choose a name for the new member of the family. Michael, Matthew, and Mitchell are being considered for first names, and Andrew, Simon, and Brian are possible middle names. What are the possible names for Lisa's new brother?

*Sample Solution:*

MICHAEL ANDREW   MATTHEW ANDREW   MITCHELL ANDREW

MICHAEL SIMON   MATTHEW SIMON   MITCHELL SIMON

MICHAEL BRIAN   MATTHEW BRIAN   MITCHELL BRIAN

**5. Find the combinations:** Beth bought a blue balloon for $.75. She gave the store clerk one dollar and received $.25 change. What are the possible combinations of quarters, dimes, and nickels she could receive for change?

*Sample Solution:*

| QUARTERS | DIMES | NICKELS | TOTAL |
|----------|-------|---------|-------|
| 1 | 0 | 0 | 25 |
| 0 | 2 | 1 | 25 |
| 0 | 1 | 3 | 25 |
| 0 | 0 | 5 | 25 |

## Extensions

**1. Simple statistics:** Use the "favorite things" graphs from the warm-up exercises to introduce simple statistics. Determine the sample size according to the number of students represented in each graph.

Discuss the data in each graph. What can be learned about the students' preferences? Using the information in the graphs, can conclusions be drawn for the class? Can valid conclusions be drawn for all students of that age in the United States?

**2. Factorials:** *3!* does not mean you should shout number three! It is read "three factorial," which in mathematical terms means: 3! = 1 x 2 x 3 = 6. For students who are ready for something extra in math, try teaching them this mathematical process for determining the number of possible combinations for varying numbers of items.

In Problem Three on page 50, the question asked students to list the different numerical combinations for two, three, and four digits. Mathematically, the number of possibilities can be computed by using factorials. Two digits is 2! or 1 x 2 = 2 possible combinations; three digits is 3! or 1 x 2 x 3 = 6 possible combinations; and four digits is 4! or 1 x 2 x 3 x 4 = 24 possible combinations. The organized lists show each possibility, while factorials give the number of possible combinations.

Have students complete this chart:

| Equation | | Total |
|---|---|---|
| 1! = 1 | = | |
| 2! = 1 x 2 | = | |
| 3! = 1 x 2 x 3 | = | |
| 4! = 1 x 2 x 3 x 4 | = | |
| 5! = 1 x 2 x 3 x 4 x 5 | = | |

Explain that 5! means that five students could arrange themselves in line in 120 different ways.

**3. Computer spreadsheets or graphs:** If you have access to a computer with spreadsheet and graphing capabilities, students can print out their own visual aids. With spreadsheets, charts with daily, weekly, and monthly average temperatures can be kept. Graphing capabilities allow students to see line, bar, and circle graphs depicting the same information in different forms.

Instructions for spreadsheets and graphs vary according to the type of software you are using. If you are not familiar with these features, ask a high school computer specialist or a community volunteer to come in and teach the students how to use these tools.

## *Draw a Picture or Use Real Objects*

Visualizing the circumstances in a problem can be very helpful. Drawing pictures or diagrams or using actual objects are ways that help students process the situation in the problem by making it more concrete. The drawings or diagrams need only be rough representations; students should not become sidetracked by making elaborate pictures. Students could draw a picture or use real objects to solve the following problem:

**Nick had 24 marbles. He gave half of them to Marty, then he gave one-third of the remaining marbles to Kate. How many marbles did Nick have left for himself?**

*Sample Solution:*

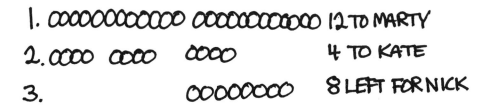

A student capable of mentally calculating this problem would use the key word *left* for subtraction, then solve the problem in his or her head. Other students would find it faster simply to solve the problem mathematically with paper and pencil. The picture or real object option should be available, though, for those students who deal better with the concrete.

## Warm-ups

**1. Making maps:** Mapping is an excellent way to integrate geography with problem solving. The picture or diagram clarifies the relationships between places and distances. Beyond math, examining maps helps students understand the role geography plays in many historical and current world events.

**2. Tangrams:** A tangram is a Chinese puzzle made by dividing a square into 5 triangles, 1 square, and 1 rhomboid (a type of parallelogram). Students can make letters, designs, and animal shapes from these challenging puzzle pieces.

**3. Geoboards:** Hands-on experience can be gained by using geoboards to make geometric shapes and designs by stretching rubberbands on the pins in the geoboards. Creative thinking is enhanced as students use a variety of designs to demonstrate the same shapes.

## Applications

**1. Find the number:** Charlie Chipmunk is gathering acorns for the coming winter. He is fortunate, because he lives on a road that is lined with oak trees. First, Charlie scampers west 3 trees to the beginning of the road. Next, he runs east 6 trees. Then, he runs west 4 trees. Finally, he dashes east 6 more trees, reaching the end of the road with a large supply of acorns. How many trees are along the road?

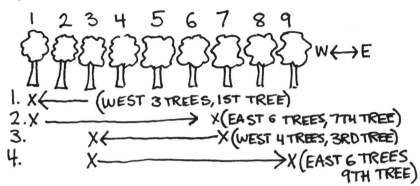

1. X⟵———— (WEST 3 TREES, 1ST TREE)
2. X ————————⟶ X (EAST 6 TREES, 7TH TREE)
3.      X⟵————————X (WEST 4 TREES, 3RD TREE)
4.      X————————⟶X (EAST 6 TREES, 9TH TREE)

**2. Draw Fred's stacks:** Finicky Fred was in charge of keeping the paper shelf neat. He was so finicky that he stacked the colored construction paper in a certain way. He made 2 equal piles of paper and insisted on putting the yellow on top of the left stack. He put the green paper under the red and above the blue. Finally, Fred put the orange above the purple and put both of these colors under the yellow. How were the 2 stacks of paper arranged?

*Sample Solution:*

| YELLOW | RED |
|--------|-------|
| ORANGE | GREEN |
| PURPLE | BLUE |

**3. Plan Tina's garden:** Tina Gardner is planting a small vegetable garden of tomatoes, beans, and peas. How can she plant her garden so that her peas are next to the beans, but not touching the tomatoes?

*Sample Solution:*

PEAS / BEANS / TOMATOES

### Extensions

**1. Studying proportion:** Have students use Cuisenaire Rods to explore relationships between sizes. Find out which ones make a 2 to 1 ratio, a 3 to 1 ratio, etc.

With older students, try analogies that show relationships between sets of numbers. Some examples:

    **a.** 6 is to 2 as 9 is to _____.      (3)
    **b.** 15 is to 5 as 12 is to _____.   (4)
    **c.** 48 is to 6 as 32 is to _____.   (4)

**2. Toothpick structures:** Hand out toothpicks and clay (to be used as mortar) for students to make structures. A few examples of problems that might be explored are: Who can make the tallest building? Who can make the longest bridge? Who can make a bridge that will support a box of crayons?

**3. Inventions:** This creative problem solving activity gives students the chance to design items that make work simpler. Students might create real things, such as desk litter baskets, or they might draw fantasy objects that only exist on paper, such as homework machines.

## Work Backwards or Make It Simpler

Sometimes problems are best solved by working backwards. Have you ever forgotten something and retraced your steps to find it? It's actually easier to begin at the end and think back. This is one way a problem can be made simpler.

Some questions might contain very large numbers or an abundance of data. Other problems might contain multiple or different units of measure such as cups and ounces, or quarts and liters, which need to be converted to one standard measure before proceeding. Simplifying before beginning can help make problems more approachable and understandable. This strategy frequently works in conjunction with others, such as making a table, list, or picture.

**Terry, Mary, and Harry decided to have a jumping contest. Terry jumped 2 feet farther than Harry. Mary jumped a total of 8 feet, which was 2 feet farther than Terry. How far did Harry jump?**

**Sample Solution:** *Working backwards helps simplify this problem: Mary jumped the farthest, a total of 8 feet. This was 2 feet more than Terry, which means Terry jumped 6 feet. Finally, we look back and find that Terry jumped 2 feet farther than Harry. Harry, therefore, jumped 4 feet.*

## Warm-ups

**1. Read aloud:** The books *How Much Is a Million?* and *If You Made a Million* by David Schwartz (listed as recommended materials in the back of this book) are motivational books which help students understand the concept of one million. In *How Much Is a Million?*, millions, billions, and trillions are explained through concrete examples that hold children in awe of how vast these numbers really are.

**2. Retracing your steps:** Ask students to work as partners in this working backwards activity. One student is the escort who plans a short walking expedition for his or her partner. Before taking the walk, the escort hides a designated object such as a walnut at one of the intended stops. The escort then takes her partner on the walk, stopping at specific locations along the way. After he arrives back at the starting place, the partner must retrace his steps and check each stop for the hidden walnut. (The concealed object must be hidden under something at the stop, not nearby.)

**3. Let's be agreeable:** Practice making things simpler by changing ounces to pounds; gallons to quarts, pints, and cups; yards to inches and feet; and days to hours, minutes, and seconds. Students should learn that the units of measure usually need to "speak the same language" before they are used in problem solving.

## Applications

**1. Find the number:** Terry, Harry, and Mary went to the carnival. They decided to see who could get the highest score at the dart throwing booth. Harry went first. His score was 5 less than Mary's. Mary's score was half as great as Terry's, who scored a total of 28 points. How much did Harry score?

> **Sample Solution:** *Working backwards from 28, you know Mary scored half of this number, or 14. Next, the problem said that Harry scored 5 less than Mary. 14 - 5 = 9*

**2. Find the number:** Sarah glued five plain wooden blocks together to make a support for her desk, which had one broken leg. She decided the blocks would look better if she painted them brown to match the desk. How many sides of the blocks will she actually need to paint?

> **Sample Solution:** *Make the problem simpler by drawing a picture (and then counting the sides that show) or making a table.*

Picture:

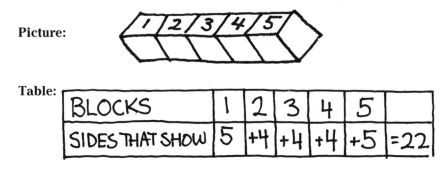

Table:

| BLOCKS | 1 | 2 | 3 | 4 | 5 | |
|---|---|---|---|---|---|---|
| SIDES THAT SHOW | 5 | +4 | +4 | +4 | +5 | =22 |

## Extensions

**1. From here to there:** In this activity, students make maps showing their routes from school and back to their homes. They should include street names, important landmarks, distances, and a legend on their maps.

**2. Codes and hidden messages:** This motivational activity has students making up codes for numbers and letters of the alphabet, then writing messages or math problems in code. They can exchange messages or problems with each other and include an answer key for the code, or they can challenge each other to first try to decipher the code, then read the message or solve the problem.

**3. Student books/*How Much Is a ???*:** Another writing activity for students is modeled on the book *How Much Is a Million?* Students can write their own books that will help others visualize and understand other numbers. Research will be necessary for students to figure out representations of their numbers. For example, *How Much Is a Hundred?* might include the example of how many inches one hundred dollar bills would stretch if they were placed end to end. The book might also share the combined average weight of one hundred students and compare it to an object of equal weight. Try a book such as *How Much Is a Meter?* to reinforce an understanding of the metric system. Include simple and complex examples, according to the developmental and ability levels of students.

## *Find a Pattern*

Patterns are widespread in the world of mathematics as well as in our everyday lives. Young students are exposed to patterns when they have set routines, when they learn to count, or when they recite their ABC's.

When students study and determine patterns, they learn to make valid predictions and generalizations. They discover the rules that govern each particular arrangement. They think about relationships that exist between numbers or things.

The following problem demonstrates how finding a pattern (by making a table) can help in finding a solution:

**Farmer Brown planted several rows of beans in late May. He was anxious to see how quickly they would grow. On Monday he checked and 5 plants had sprouted. On Tuesday, he discovered 10**

new plants, and on Wednesday, there were 15. If the beans continue sprouting at this rate, how many new plants will appear on Sunday?

*Sample Solution:*

pattern rule: multiples of 5

| MON. | TUES. | WED. | THURS. | FRI | SAT. | SUN. |
|------|-------|------|--------|-----|------|------|
| 5 | 10 | 15 | 20 | 25 | 30 | 35 |

## Warm-Ups

**1. Finding patterns around us:** Look around the classroom and list the different patterns found in the room. Window panes, ceiling or floor tiles, alphabet charts, and calendars are but a few possibilities you might encounter. Try going into the school yard and checking for patterns in nature or the equipment and buildings near the school.

**2. Things we can count on:** List the various natural events we can count on. Sunrise, sunset, low tide, high tide, stages of the moon, and constellations are some of the possible responses. Ask students if they have daily patterns or routines they follow. Invite them to share and compare.

**3. Making bead bracelets:** Using string and multicolored beads, make bracelets that show color patterns. Share the completed bracelets and ask students to identify the pattern rule for each one.

## Applications

**1. Continue the pattern:**

    **a.** 2, 4, 6, _____, _____ (8, 10; pattern rule: multiples of two)
    **b.** Ann, Beth, Cathy, _____, _____ (Debbie, Eleanor; pattern rule: girls' names in alphabetical order, each name increasing by one letter.)

**c.** 1, 5, 3, 7, _____, _____ (5, 9; pattern rule: add four, subtract two)

**d.** 2, 10, 7, 35, 32, _____, _____ (160, 157; pattern rule: multiply by five, subtract three)

**e.** A, 1, C, 3, E, 5, _____, _____ (G, 7; pattern rule: every other letter of the alphabet beginning with A, alternating with odd numbers beginning with 1)

**2. Find the number:** If Ruby puts 2 rocks in her collection on the first day, 5 on the second, and 8 on the third, how many rocks will she have in her collection on the seventh day?

*Sample Solution:*

**pattern rule: add 3**

| 1ST | 2ND | 3RD | 4TH | 5TH | 6TH | 7TH | TOTAL |
|---|---|---|---|---|---|---|---|
| 2 | +5 | +8 | +11 | +14 | +17 | +20 | =77 ROCKS |

**3. Find the number:** A subway beginning its morning run picked up 2 people at the first stop, 4 at the second, and 6 at the third. At this rate, how many people got on the subway at the tenth stop?

*Sample Solution:*

**pattern rule: add two**

| STOP | 1 | 2 | 3 | 4 | 5 | 6 | 7 | 8 | 9 | 10← |
|---|---|---|---|---|---|---|---|---|---|---|
| PEOPLE | 2 | 4 | 6 | 8 | 10 | 12 | 14 | 16 | 18 | 20← |

## Extensions

**1. Designing tessellations:** Tessellations are designs made up of geometric shapes, where colors frequently accentuate the patterns. A variety of publishers offer books of tessellations, that are reproducible so students can color them. I have learned that students themselves enjoy making their own designs for others to color. It is a great art project to integrate with studying geometry and patterns in problem solving. A class booklet can be made containing the students' best tessellations.

**2. Palindromes:** Numbers that read the same forward and backward, such as 353, are palindromes. Some words, including madam and eye, are palindromes, too. For an enrichment activity, ask students to list all the palindromes from one to one hundred. Another suggestion is to try a cooperative learning lesson, where the groups make lists of as many word palindromes as possible during a set period of time.

**3. Patterns worth watching:** Patterns play an important role in many professions. A financial analyst must watch business trends and fluctuations in the stock market. A meteorologist studies weather patterns when preparing forecasts, and a city planner might study traffic patterns to solve the problem of rush hour congestion.

Discuss other examples of professions that rely on patterns and how their use can help solve problems. Perhaps the class could study a problem facing the school, such as student traffic at lunch or recess. Real-life situations help students see a problem through its stages of identification, planning, and resolution.

## Use Logic

Logical thinking exercises help students learn to use the process of elimination or deductive thinking to arrive at a solution. Most problems present a variety of conditions and students must use an "if . . . then" thinking approach. It is important that students read the entire problem first, then choose the best clue for starting. Making a chart or drawing a picture are good strategies when practicing logic with reasoning. The following problem calls for the use of logic in its solution:

**Max, Meg, and Mike decided to go to Joan's Cones for ice cream, where each chose one of the three flavors, vanilla, chocolate, or**

strawberry. Using the following clues, who ordered which flavor?

a. Meg never eats anything that is spelled with a double letter.
b. Max loves ice cream, but wishes he were not allergic to fruits with seeds.
c. Mike said he would settle for whatever flavor was left.

*Sample Solution:*

| PERSON | VANILLA | CHOCOLATE | STRAWBERRY |
|--------|---------|-----------|------------|
| MAX | YES | NO | NO |
| MEG | NO | YES | NO |
| MIKE | NO | NO | YES |

## Warm-ups

**1. What am I?:** This is a large group game, where one person thinks of an object or an animal, then gives oral clues about its physical characteristics. Other students try to identify the mystery object or animal in the riddle based on the clues. For example: "Most people like me for about one day, then they cast me aside. I am black, white, and "read," although sometimes I might have a touch of other colors on special days. Even though I don't hang around long, you might see me again as something entirely different. What am I? (a newspaper)

**2. Category game:** This game is one of my students' favorites. I choose a category, such as things that begin with "s," without divulging it to the students. Then I say, "Finicky Fred likes the sun, but he doesn't like light. He likes seats, but not chairs, and he likes sailing, but not the water." Students do not tell me the rule, but they must give an example of what he likes and doesn't like. We play this game throughout the day when we have a few minutes of extra time. Each day we play, I change what Finicky Fred likes. The more students play, the more fine-tuned their thought processes become in identifying the rule in the riddle.

**3. Read a mystery aloud:** Choose an appropriate mystery for your class as a read aloud book, and keep a running record of the clues. Before beginning each reading session, discuss the case and make predictions based on the information gathered to date.

## Applications

**1. Which section?:** Amy, Annie, and Allie are all avid readers. When they go to the library, one girl immediately heads for the mystery section. Another goes to the science aisle, and the third stops to browse at the new selections in fantasy. Annie is quite a collector, and she especially likes unusual rocks. Allie's bedroom walls are filled with posters of dragons and mythical beasts and characters, and Amy loves to play the game of "Clue." Which section of the library do you think each girl likes best?

*Sample Solution:*

| PERSON | MYSTERY | SCIENCE | FANTASY |
|--------|---------|---------|---------|
| AMY | YES-"CLUE" | NO | NO |
| ANNIE | NO | YES· ROCKS | NO |
| ALLIE | NO | NO | YES ·POSTERS |

**2. What order?:** Tootie Fruitie loves fruit juices. She bought five bottles of juice, including apple, orange, cranberry, grape, and pineapple, and lined them up on a shelf. Use the following clues to decide the order of the bottles.
   **a.** The grape juice is in the center.
   **b.** The cranberry is to the left of the orange juice.
   **c.** The apple is on the left end of the line.

*Sample Solution: Start with clue 1 and put the grape in the center. Next, if the cranberry is to the left of the orange, and the apple is on one end, the orange has to be at the right end. By process of elimination, the pineapple will go between the apple and grape.*

# APPLE·PINEAPPLE·GRAPE·CRANBERRY·ORANGE

**3. What's the price?:** There are two sizes of laundry soap on the store shelf.

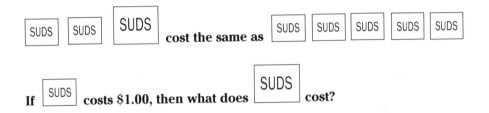

*Sample Solution: Use "if...then" thinking. If one small box is $1.00, then five small boxes must cost $5.00. Next, look at the left side of the diagram, there are two small boxes and one large box. They must cost $5.00 altogether. If two small boxes cost $2.00, the large box must cost $3.00.*

## Extensions

**1. Students' own logic problems:** Logic problems are generally favorites of students. It seems they panic when they are first exposed to them; then they cannot seem to do enough of them. After students have worked through several deductive thinking problems, ask them to write their own during writing process. On the following page is an example of a third grader's deductive thinking problem (she loves dogs!).

# DIFFERENT DOGS

Ronald Retriever, Harry Hound, Billy Beagle, Sammy Setter, and David Dalmatian all have a different breeds of dogs. One has a golden retriever, one has a basset hound, one has a beagle, one has an Irish setter, and one has a dalmatian.

**a.** David Dalmatian and Ronald Retriever have dogs with no black coloring.
**b.** Sammy Setter and Billy Beagle have dogs that are afraid of fire engines.
**c.** Sammy Setter and Ronald Retriever have dogs with no red coloring.
**d.** Billy Beagle has a dog with HUGE ears.

Who has which kind of dog?

**2. Writing mysteries:** Once you have read a mystery aloud, some students may choose to write their own as long-term writing projects. Generally, it is helpful for students to make outlines of their stories, showing the sequence of events and the unravelling of clues before beginning to write.

**3. Cartoon mysteries:** Students with artistic strengths might illustrate a comic book mystery, where the pictures play an important role in developing the characters, plot, and discovery of clues.

## *Putting the Strategies to Work*

Once students have learned the separate strategies and practiced using them individually, they are ready to work on problems that require the implementation of one or more strategies. You probably noted that pictures and tables help identify patterns, and charts definitely are useful when doing logic problems. A collection of problems ranging in difficulty from simple to complex is included in Chapter Four. Students are now ready to put the entire problem solving model to the test.

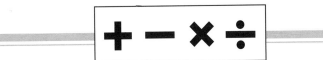

## CHAPTER FOUR
# APPLYING THE STRATEGIES:
## PROBLEM SOLVING ACTIVITIES

## A Collection of Problems for Students to Solve

Now that students have learned and practiced using the different strategies, they are ready to solve problems where they must decide what to do. In many cases, more than one strategy can be used. Students may use different approaches to problems so long as their explanations and answers are logical.

**1.** Katie is making a quilt for her doll. She wants her quilt to have 3 green patches, 3 red patches, and 3 yellow patches. How can she sew the patches so she has a green, a red, and a yellow patch in each row and in each column of her quilt?

**Strategy:** draw a picture or use real objects

*Sample Solution:*

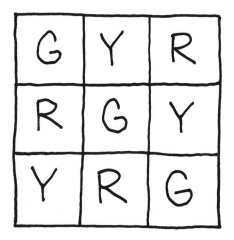

**2.** Mike had a marble collection. He wouldn't tell anyone how many he had, but he did give these clues:

  **a.** There were more than 28.
  **b.** There were fewer than 56.
  **c.** The number could only be divided evenly by 7, 1, and itself.

**Strategy:** make a table

*Sample Solution:*

| NUMBER | 28 | 35 | 42 | 49 | 56 |
|---|---|---|---|---|---|
| DIVISIBLE BY 1 AND 7 AND ITSELF | NO | NO | NO | YES ↑ | NO |

**3.** Amy was picking up litter. She gathered a total of 35 pieces of trash. Interestingly, there were only bottles and candy wrappers in her bag. If she had 9 more bottles than candy wrappers, how many of each did she have?

**Strategies:** guess and check and make a table

*Sample Solution:*

| OBJECT | 1ST | 2ND | 3RD |
|---|---|---|---|
| BOTTLES | 20 | 21 | 22 |
| CANDY WRAPPERS | 11 | 12 | 13 |
| TOTAL OF 35 | NO | NO | YES ← |
| BOTTLES 9 > CANDY WRAPPERS | YES | YES | YES ← |

**4.** Sam went with his family to the beach for a week. Each day, he would look for shells. On the first day, he found 3. On the second day, he found only 1, but on the third day, he picked up 4. He was disappointed on the fourth day when he only found 2 shells. At this rate, how many shells did Sam have in all on the seventh day?

**Strategies:** find a pattern and make a table

**Sample Solution:**

| 1ST | 2ND | 3RD | 4TH | 5TH | 6TH | 7TH | TOTAL |
|-----|-----|-----|-----|-----|-----|-----|-------|
| 3 | 1 | 4 | 2 | 5 | 3 | 6 | 24 |

**5.** Sarah lived on a lake, where wild ducks were swimming. Two ducks flew off within five minutes. Three times as many flew off after ten minutes. If there were 18 ducks at the beginning, how many were left now?

**Strategy:** work backwards

**Sample Solution:** *18 - 2 - (3 x 2) = 10*

**6.** Harry, Terry, and Mary were running in a race. Harry finished in 2 minutes. Terry finished in 110 seconds, and Mary completed it in 2 minutes and 5 seconds. How many total seconds did the three of them take to run the race?

**Strategies:** make it simpler and make a table

**Sample Solution:**

| PERSON | HARRY | TERRY | MARY | TOTAL |
|--------|-------|-------|------|-------|
| SECONDS | 2×60=120 | 110 | (2×60)+5=125 | 355 |

**7.** Wendy, Randy, Mandy, and Candy went out for pizza one evening. They sat in a booth next to a window. Can you tell who was sitting where based on the following clues?

  **a.** Candy sat across from her brother.
  **b.** Wendy reached down from where she was sitting and picked up a penny in the aisle.

**c.** Wendy handed the penny to the boy sitting next to her.

**Strategies:** use logic and draw a picture

*Sample Solution:*

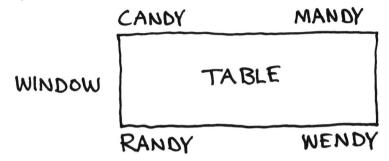

CANDY          MANDY

WINDOW      TABLE

RANDY          WENDY

**8.** The Bruisers beat the Hawks in a football game, 18 to 0. If there were no 2-point conversions or safeties in the game, what are the possible ways the Bruisers could have earned their points? (Each touchdown is 6 points, each field goal is 3 points, and a successful kick after the touchdown is 1 point.)

**Strategy:** make an organized list

*Sample Solution:*

| TOUCHDOWNS | EXTRA KICK | FIELD GOALS |
|------------|------------|-------------|
| 3          | 0          | 0           |
| 2          | 0          | 2           |
| 1          | 0          | 4           |
| 0          | 0          | 6           |

**9.** The Phrog family was having a jumping contest. Phyllis Phrog jumped 50 centimeters farther than Phil Phrog. Frank Phrog jumped a total of 2 meters, which was 1 meter farther than Phyllis jumped.  How many cenimeters did Phil Phrog jump?

**Strategies:**  make it simpler, work backwards, and draw a picture

*Sample Solution:*

 **a.** *Make it simpler by changing meters to centimeters.*

$$2 \text{ METERS} = 200 \text{ CENTIMETERS}$$
$$1 \text{ METER} = 100 \text{ CENTIMETERS}$$

 **b.** *Work backwards and draw a picture.*

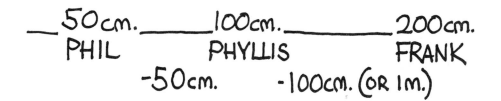

## *Climbing to Higher Levels of Problem Solving*

Students have now had a fair amount of practice applying their arithmetic skills and problem solving strategies.  Now it is time to move on to longer, more complex problems.

Perhaps the examples of case studies in Chapter Five will give you ideas for your own guided thinking activities.

## CHAPTER FIVE
# MOVING ON WITH PROBLEM SOLVING:
## GUIDED THINKING ACTIVITIES

## What Are Guided Thinking Activities?

The case studies that follow can also be called guided thinking activities. They are fictional stories which include problems to be solved. Students are not told what the problem is; instead they must analyze the situations in the stories by recognizing and identifying the key issue(s). Each case has varied, but limited information that calls for both mathematical and logical reasoning.

Using only the facts presented in the case, students suggest possible solutions for the problem(s) presented in the story. After an in-depth examination of the alternatives, the students recommend a logical plan of action.

As in real-life situations, there can be more than one correct answer. Sometimes there are better ones. The emphasis is on the logical application of facts presented in each case. Students must recognize the issues, analyze the given information, then suggest a reasonable plan of action.

When students work on activities such as these, they are not passive witnesses to a problem as it is being worked out but instead are active participants in the process. Guided thinking activities provide an opportunity for students to use the thinking skills and problem solving strategies they have learned.

## Presenting the Case

How are case studies presented to the class? The first time I present a case, I do it with the whole class. After the introductory lesson, the students work on cases in cooperative learning groups.

The problem solving model presented in Chapter Two is similar to that used for the cases. Each step will be more complex, however, and will require more time and thought. I give the groups a designated amount of time to complete each step in the problem solving model; then we discuss their results before moving to the next level. In other words, the teacher serves as a guide through the thinking process.

Calculators should be used, if possible, in order to save time doing lengthy computations. Along with their math calculations, students should also use their common sense and logic to determine possible solutions for the problem.

## Choosing a Plan of Action

On the board, list and examine all reasonable options that the groups have presented. Then ask whether there is a plan of action that is better than all others, or are all options equally feasible? Remind the class that in life, we face many kinds of decisions where we might choose a variety of alternatives. Sometimes there are better ones, or even a best option. We should just be sure that option is reasonable.

### THE CASE OF THE SCATTERBRAIN TRAVEL AGENCY

Mr. B.A. Scatterbrain owns a travel agency in New York City, and he was having one of those days where everything seems to go wrong. Closing time was at 5:00 p.m., and it was already 4:30. An unbelievable catastrophe had happened.

Three customers had been in that day to plan trips. He remembered the people were M.C. Wrench, C. Fisher, and Michael Michaels, who also had his son with him. Mr. Scatterbrain remembered that one customer wanted to go to Tampa, another to Boston, and the third to Los Angeles. He also recalled that each insisted on a different kind of travel: air, train, and rental car. He remembered all this, but could not recall who wanted to go where and how they wanted to get there.

Mr. Scatterbrain was much too embarrassed to call the people, so he sat down, sighed, and carefully thought back over the day. He could picture Mr. Michaels and his son Michael, Jr. The little boy was so excited about going to Disneyworld . . . or was it Disneyland? It was one of the two.

Then he remembered that M.C. Wrench requested a window seat away from the wing, and he wanted a vegetarian meal instead of the regular dinner. He found M.C. Wrench rather peculiar, because he was so interested in traveling to see a bunch of sheep play, or *rams* as he called them.

Mr. Scatterbrain continued to concentrate on what he could remember. C. Fisher said something about getting out of the office and out on the open water. She couldn't wait to eat some fresh seafood, especially a baked scrod dinner. She mentioned needing some maps of the state capital since she had not driven there in a long time. Oh yes, something was said about stopping in New Haven to visit an old friend.

B.A. Scatterbrain glanced up at the clock. It was 4:45 p.m.; in fifteen minutes his three clients would be in to pick up their tickets. Can you help Mr. Scatterbrain straighten out this mess? He would surely appreciate it!

## Addressing the Problem

1. **Problem:** Mr. Scatterbrain must figure out where his three clients are going and how they are getting there.

2. **Facts:** He remembered several comments that are clues:

   **a.** The Michaels wanted to go to Disneyworld or Disneyland.
   **b.** M.C. Wrench wanted a window seat away from the wing, a vegetarian dinner, and he was looking forward to watching a bunch of sheep or rams play.
   **c.** C. Fisher wanted to get out on the water and have a baked scrod dinner. She needed maps of the state capital, and she was going to stop in New Haven along the way. She had not driven there in a long time.

3. **Strategy:** Make a chart and use logic.

|  | MR. MICHAELS | M.C. WRENCH | C. FISHER |
|---|---|---|---|
| BOSTON |  |  | YES<br>STATE CAPITAL |
| TAMPA | YES - PROCESS OF ELIMINATION AND CLOSE TO DISNEY WORLD |  |  |
| LOS ANGELES |  | YES - THE L.A. RAMS ARE HERE |  |
| AIRPLANE |  | YES - WANTED WINDOW SEAT AWAY FROM WING |  |
| TRAIN | YES - PROCESS OF ELIMINATION |  |  |
| RENTAL CAR |  |  | YES - HAD NOT DRIVEN IN A WHILE. STOPPING IN NEW HAVEN |

**4. Plan of action:** Even though the clues are not definitive, do students feel the options are logical enough for Mr. Scatterbrain to prepare train tickets to Tampa for Mr. Michaels, an airplane ticket for M.C. Wrench to Los Angeles, and a rental car agreement for C. Fisher to drive to Boston? Have students discuss and decide what B.A. Scatterbrain should do. He and the students have fifteen minutes to decide.

### THE CASE OF THE UNFINISHED SECOND FLOOR

183 Elm Street was the address for the two-story home of the Williams family. They bought the house two years ago for a very low price because it needed many repairs.

In fact, the second floor needed to be completely refinished.  It was just one large empty space, rectangular in shape and measuring 30 feet by 20 feet.

The family had been living on the first floor for the past two years and was feeling quite cramped.  In just one month, Grandma Williams was going to move in with the family, so it was time to do something about the upstairs.

The family sat down and it was decided that the two older sons, Jack, 13, and Bill, 11, would help design the new second floor.  Mr. and Mrs. Williams were both handy and planned on doing the work themselves.

When the family held their planning session, they had a few important factors to consider.  They would need to divide the space into 4 rooms.  One room would be a bathroom and the other 3 rooms would be bedrooms.

Grandma would need to be right next to the bathroom.  One-year-old Mickey had to be next to the bathroom, too, but couldn't be next to Grandma's room.  His waking and crying in the night might disturb the elderly woman.  Jack and Bill would room together.  They figured they would need a room at least 13 feet by 12 feet to give themselves enough space.  The stairway ended right in the middle of the 30-foot side of the room.

The family decided to plan on a 4-foot hallway dividing the two sides of the upstairs.  There would be 2 large rooms of the same size and 2 smaller rooms of the same size.  The boys would automatically get one of the large rooms because they needed the space.

The family struggled trying to decide what should be done about the other 3 rooms. Can you help the Williams family? After all, Grandma will be here in no time.

## Addressing the Problem

**1. Problem:** What should the room assignments be for the second floor?

**2. Facts:** The important things to remember are:

   **a.** The space measures 30 feet by 20 feet.
   **b.** The staircase ends in the middle of the 30 foot length.
   **c.** The hallway will be 4 feet wide and start at the staircase.
   **d.** The boys will have one of the large rooms that will measure 13 feet by 12 feet.

**3. Conditions:** Grandma must be next to the bathroom, but not next to little Mickey.

**4. Strategy:** Draw a picture, work backwards, and use logic. Draw a rectangular shape and label the length 30 feet and the width 20 feet. Working backwards, show a staircase in the middle of the 30-foot wall. Extend a 4-foot hallway to the opposite side.

Next show the room dimensions of 13 feet on either side of the hall. The boys must have a room 13 by 12 feet, so sketch another wall to form 2 opposite rooms that are 13 by 12. That leaves two other opposite rooms, both 13 by 8 feet.

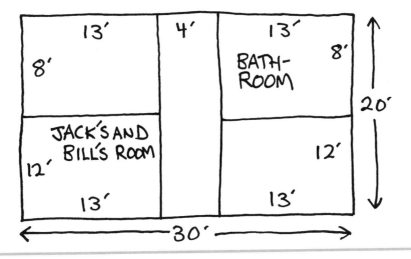

**5. Plan of action:** The rooms are now set, but a dilemma remains. Grandma and Mickey cannot be next to each other, and they both need to be next to the bathroom, which means one of them will get a large room and the other will get the small one.

It is at this point groups may differ in their opinions. They should decide whether Grandma or Mickey should be in the large room and back up their opinions with logical reasons.

The older boys' room is set. It is one of the 13 by 12 foot rooms. The bathroom must be diagonally across from theirs in one of the 13 by 8 rooms. The other two rooms' occupants are open to debate.

## THE MELVILLE LAND CASE

The city of Melville grew rapidly in the 1980's. The economy prospered thanks to Ellen J. Barlett, an entrepreneur who started a computer software business which provided many jobs for residents. The city was picturesque and was situated by a large lake, which was popular for fishing and boating.

The residents of Melville took great pride in their city. They had strict laws to protect the environment. Recently, a law was passed that required any new building be built on at least one acre of land.

Many people moved into Melville. One result of this was the lack of space for new buildings. Recently, the economy took a turn for the worse. Now there were too many people and not enough jobs. Several people were laid off and looking for work. Times were hard.

In Melville, there was a parcel of land 200 feet by 200 feet. It was the city playground for the kids. Each day, many children came to play ball, swing, or just plain have fun.

At the next city planning meeting, two new faces were in the crowd. James R. Smith represented Big R Burgers, who wanted to purchase the playground land to build a fast food restaurant. Nancy K. Swan was also there for Water Slide Mania, and she wanted to buy the land to construct a water park.

Many kids and their parents heard about these proposals. They showed up at the next meeting, because they did not want to lose their only playground.

The Melville City planners are not sure what to do. Help them look at each option and make a wise decision.

## Addressing the Problem

1. **Problem:** Should the playground remain as it is, be sold to Big R Burgers, or be sold to Water Slide Mania?

2. **Facts:** The important things to remember are:
   a. The town is facing hard economic times.
   b. The land in question is Melville's only playground.

3. **Conditions:** Any new building must be put on at least one acre of land. The playground is 200 by 200 feet, which equals 40,000 square feet. An acre is 43,560 square feet. This eliminates the Big R Burger Restaurant.

4. **Strategy:** Make a table or an organized list and use logic.

| POSSIBILITIES | PROS | CONS |
|---|---|---|
| PLAYGROUND | | |
| WATER SLIDE MANIA | | |

5. **Plan of action:** With Big R Burgers eliminated, students must decide whether the land should remain a playground or be sold to Water Slide

Mania. Once pros and cons have been listed for both options, ask students to examine them critically, then discuss the comments. Take a class vote for Melville.

## Integrating Writing Process with Case Studies

Students truly demonstrate thinking when they not only solve complex problems, but write examples of case studies themselves. During one quarter out of each year math is the focus of our writing time. Many students choose to do case studies. An example written by a fourth grader with her own thoughts for the solution is included below:

---

### JOE'S SUMMER JOB

The life of Joe Smith was an active one. Every minute of the day he was either doing a sport or some kind of exercise. (Joe was always outside.) As time went on and he grew, Joe decided that he needed a summer job (He needed some extra money to buy some more sports equipment.) He had seen a lot of things in magazines that he liked. But the three things he liked best were:

**a.** A new bike at the amazing price of $220.00
**b.** A new pool table for $596.00
**c.** And last of all a Nintendo entertainment center with two games for $99.00.

The job offers he got were:

**1.** Working behind the counter at the Bike Shop for $3.00 an hour. He would work there for three days a week. He would be working there for three hours a day.
**2.** Working at the grocery store packing bags for $5.00 an hour. He would work packing bags for three days a week and for four hours a day.
**3.** And being a camp counselor for two weeks in the summer. He would receive $125.00 a week.

By knowing what Joe likes to do, can you figure out what job he should take and what to buy with his money?

---

## *Real-life Case Studies*

Many real-life problems are not resolved quickly and require varied amounts of time. A long-term plan is devised where data are collected and studied, then decisions or generalizations are made. A good example is a science experiment that tests the effect of water on plant growth. The problem is identified, materials necessary to conduct the study are gathered, then students observe, record, and study the results before making generalizations.

Along with the fictitious case study method, examining real-life situations is a valuable experience. Almost any group, whether business or recreational, faces issues it must resolve. Students, too, can participate actively in a move to solving process. The model I use for real problems is very similar to the one for math questions:

1. Determine the problem you will study.
2. Identify the types of information that need to be gathered to study the problem.
3. Specify any conditions that must be considered.
4. Collect and record data.
5. Organize and analyze the data and problem.
6. Make recommendations.

How do you choose a real-life problem to study? There are as many possibilities as there are classrooms, but some suggestions are:

1. How can the class get the school to "think metric?"

2. What could be done to make the school grounds more attractive?

3. If the class wants to take care of a pet, what preparatory steps should be taken? What will the long-term costs and responsibilities be?

4. How nutritious is the school menu? Study it on a weekly or monthly basis for nutritional value. How much waste is there from each type of meal? How could determining high-waste meals be helpful to the food service department?

**5.** Is there a recycling system in your building? If there is, how effective is it? If one does not exist, what would be necessary to set up such a program?

**6.** What is the temperature pattern in your area? Has it remained the same, decreased, or increased over the past ten years? Go to the library to research the topic. Graph and share your findings. Can generalizations be made?

**7.** Study the growth rate in your school, town, or city. How has it changed over the past five years? What are the implications of your findings?

**8.** What's a person to believe? Analyze the ads on television and conduct your own studies.

- Test which batteries last longest.
- Conduct a taste test of two popular beverages.
- Check to see which paper towels are strongest.
- Research to find out which cars are safest.

**9.** Call the town or city office or a local organization and ask if they have an issue your class might help study. It would give kids an opportunity to experience the entire process and see the frustrations that arise in group problem solving.

**10.** Compare temperature and precipitation of your town with another in a different part of the country. Graph your findings. Do any patterns emerge?

## Becoming Active Problem Solvers

Experience has taught me that kids love a challenge. Problem solving should be an integral part of their day. When given the necessary tools and opportunities, students can become lifelong problem solvers.

# Recommended Materials

## Children's Books:

Base, Graeme. *The Eleventh Hour.* New York: Harry N. Abrams, Inc., 1989.

Schwartz, David M. *How Much Is a Million?* New York: Lothrop, Lee, & Shepard Books, 1985.

Schwartz, David M. *If You Made a Million.* New York: Lothrop, Lee, & Shepard Books, 1989.

## Problem Solving Books:

Brumbaugh, Allyne. *Do-It-Yourself Math Stories.* New York: Scholastic, 1992.

Burns, Marilyn. *A Collection of Math Lessons from Grades 3 Through 6.* New York: The Math Solution Publications, 1987.

Burns, Marilyn. *Math for Smarty Pants.* Boston: Little, Brown, & Co., 1982.

Schoenfield, Mark and Jeannette Rosenblatt. *Discovering Logic.* Bellmont, CA: David S. Lake Publishers, 1985.

Schoenfield, Mark and Jeannette Rosenblatt. *Playing With Logic.* Belmont, CA: David S. Lake Publishers, 1985.

Seymour, Dale. *Problem Parade.* Palo Alto, CA: Dale Seymour Publications, 1984.

Vydra, Joan and Jean McCall. *No Problem!* San Luis Obispo, CA: Dandy Lion Publications, 1989.

## Professional Books:

*Curriculum and Evaluation: Standards for School Mathematics.* Reston, VA: National Council of Teachers of Mathematics, Inc., 1989.

Ellis, Susan S. and Susan F. Whalen. *Cooperative Learning: Getting Started.* New York: Scholastic, 1990.